I CAN SEE PLANET RS FROM MY ROOM! HOW THE TELESCOPE WORKS

PHYSICS BOOK 4TH GRADE CHILDREN'S PHYSICS BOOKS

BABY PROFESSOR
EDUCATION KIDS

Speedy Publishing LLC

40 E. Main St. #1156

Newark, DE 19711

www.speedypublishing.com

Copyright 2017

In this book, we're going to talk about how you can see planets and stars from your room by using a telescope and becoming an amateur astronomer. So, let's get right to it!

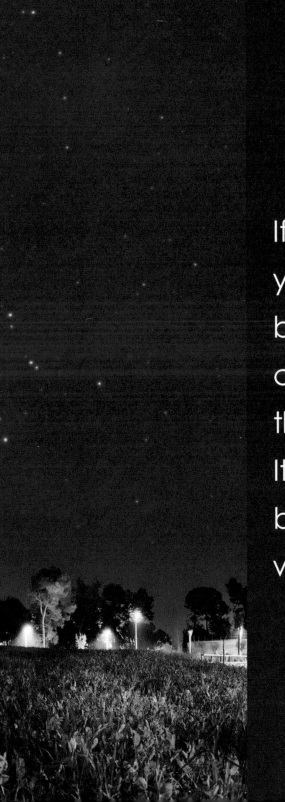

If you have a telescope, you can point it outside your bedroom window and you can see planets and stars that are millions of miles away. It almost seems like magic, but telescopes work the same way your eyes do.

They just magnify planets and stars many times so that you can see them more clearly. The science that is used to create telescopes is used in binoculars as well as cameras.

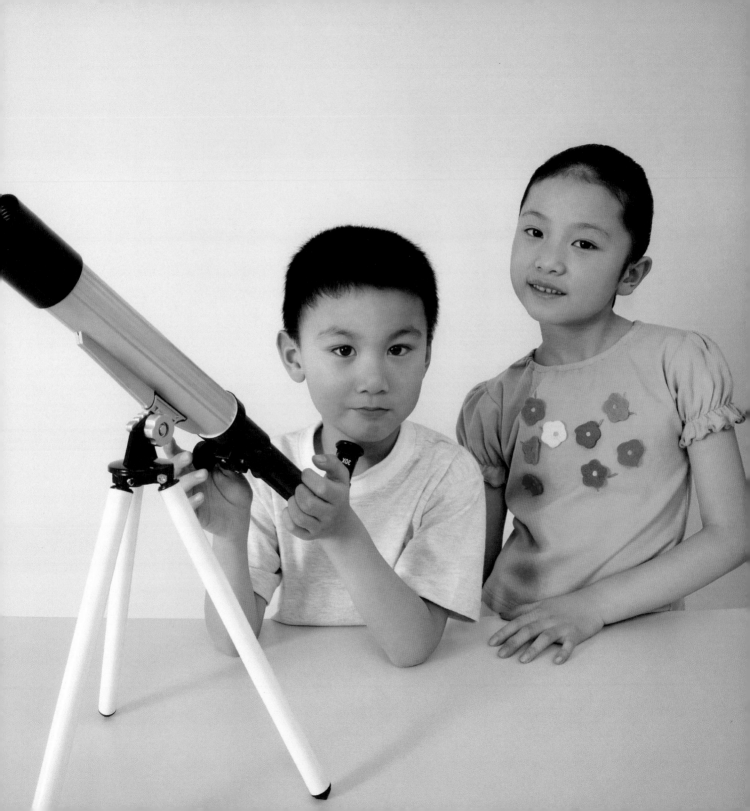

HISTORY OF THE TELESCOPE

For thousands of years, men and women looked up at the sky and they could see the moon, a few planets that were visible to the naked eye, and stars. The telescope was eventually invented in 1608 AD and that changed everything!.

Hans Lippershey, a Dutch lensmaker, was interested in making far away things look like they were up close. His experiments with lenses led to the first refracting telescope, but at that time the telescope was used for surveying and for seeing land from ships. No one had thought to point it up at planets and stars.

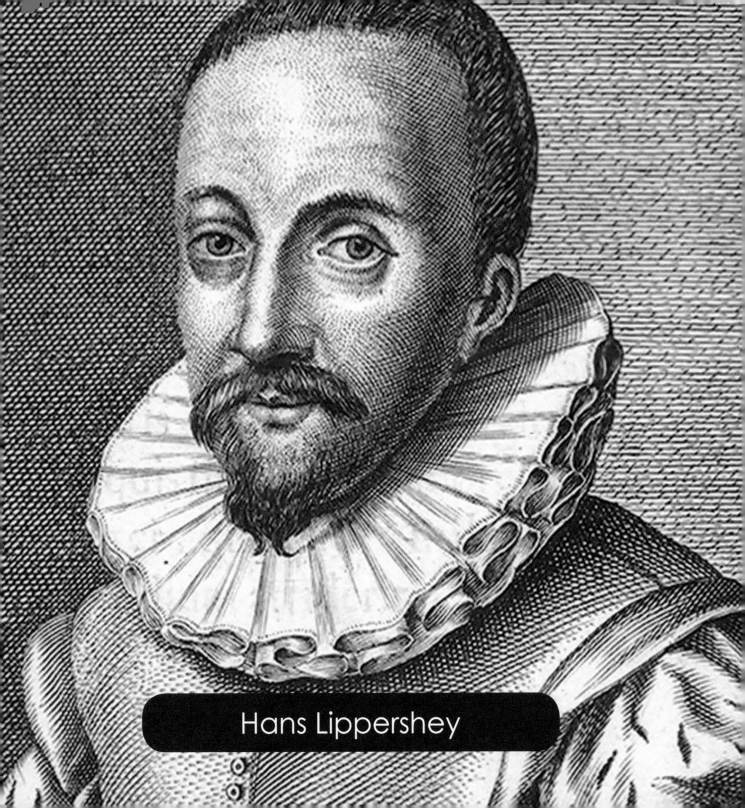

Hans Lippershey

Galileo Galilei

In 1610, the Italian astronomer Galileo Galilei built his own refracting telescope based on the Dutch inventions and then added his own improvements to the device. He was the first to use a telescope to view celestial bodies.

He wrote a book about his findings called "The Starry Messenger." In the book, Galileo outlines his observations of the craters on the moon, the moons of Jupiter, and the stars in the Milky Way. Galileo's book made him very famous and soon important people were flocking to him in the hopes that he would name some of the heavenly bodies he saw after them.

Galileo Demonstrating the New Astronomical Theories at the University of Padua.

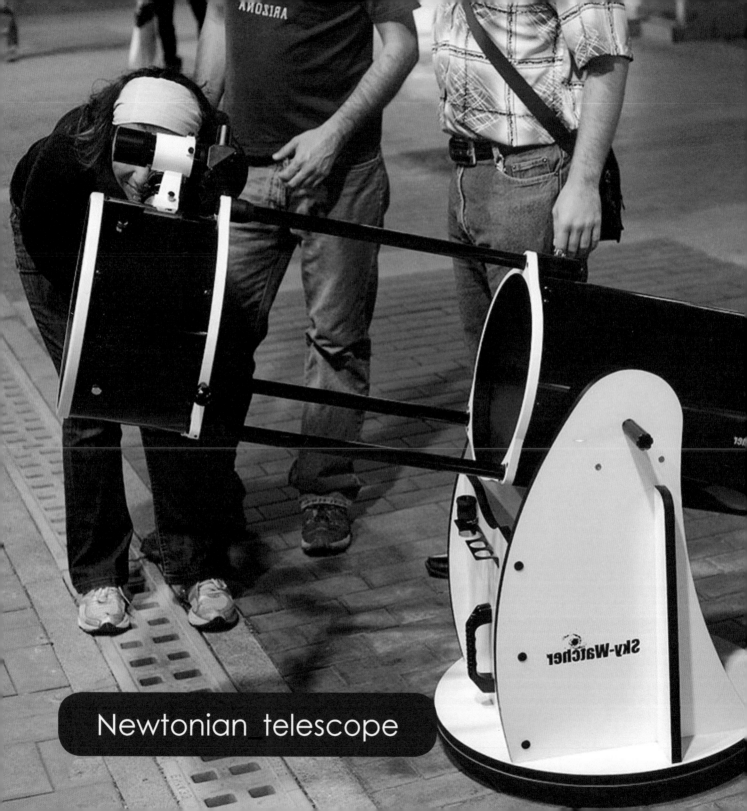

Newtonian_telescope

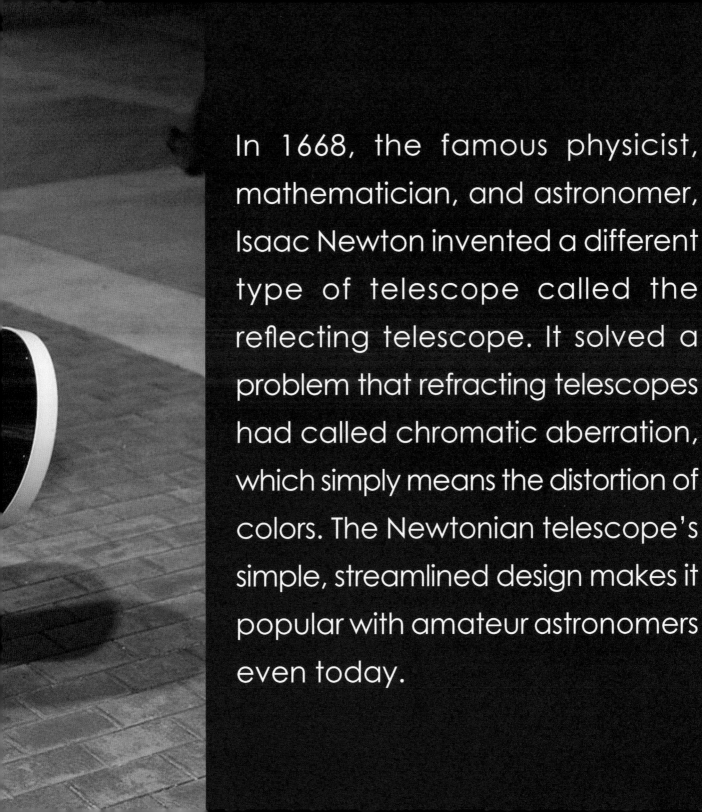

In 1668, the famous physicist, mathematician, and astronomer, Isaac Newton invented a different type of telescope called the reflecting telescope. It solved a problem that refracting telescopes had called chromatic aberration, which simply means the distortion of colors. The Newtonian telescope's simple, streamlined design makes it popular with amateur astronomers even today.

A TELESCOPE'S PROPERTIES

A telescope has two properties that are very important. The size of its aperture, which is the opening where light comes in, determines how well it can gather rays of light. The larger the aperture, the more light it can gather, and the better you'll be able to see far-away objects in the night sky.

Man looking skyward through Astronomical telescope

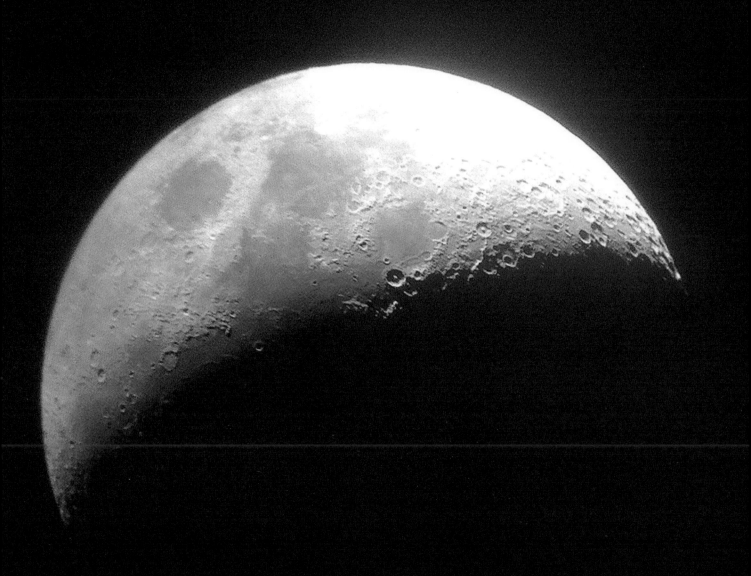

The Moon seen from a Telescope

The second property is how well it magnifies. The telescope's magnification will tell you how much larger it will make the objects you're viewing appear.

REFRACTING AND REFLECTING

The first type of telescope invented was a refracting telescope. It uses lenses to make images larger. The second type of telescope invented was the reflecting telescope, which uses mirrors. It's easy to remember which telescope uses lenses and which uses mirrors if you think of it this way:

- ⮒ Refracting telescope, uses lenses to bend or refract

- ⮒ Reflecting telescope, uses mirrors to reflect

Reflecting Telescope

Milky Way

THE PATH OF LIGHT

A telescope gathers light and also focuses it. Before you can understand how a telescope works, you have to have a basic understanding of how our eyes work. Let's use the light from just one star to talk about this. As the light rays from a distant star travel to Earth they spread out.

As an observer on Earth, only some of the rays go into the pupils of your eyes. The pupil is the dark circle in your eye that is the opening into the lens of your eye, just as the aperture of a telescope is to the telescope's lens or mirror.

Human Eye

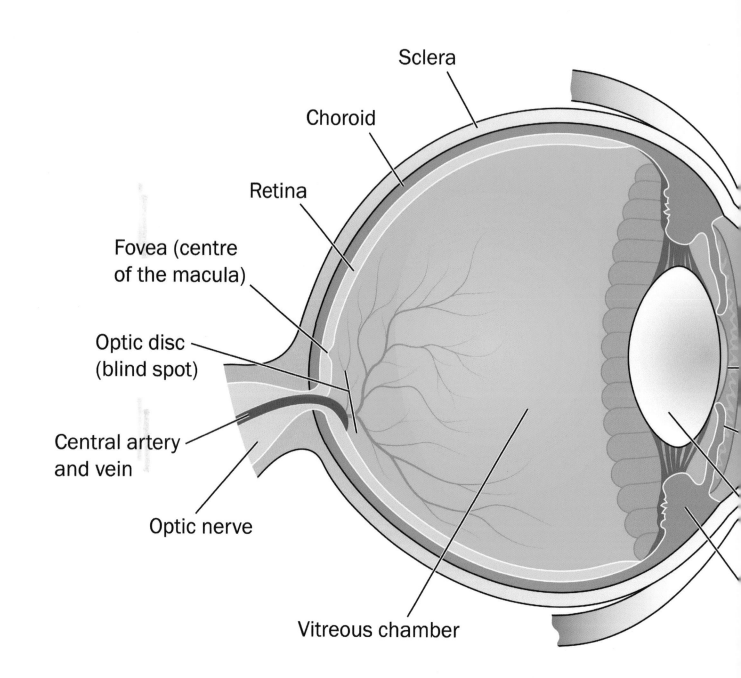

Sclera

Choroid

Retina

Fovea (centre
of the macula)

Optic disc
(blind spot)

Central artery
and vein

Optic nerve

Vitreous chamber

njunctiva

Cornea

Pupil

Iris

ody

As the light rays pass through the pupil of your eye, the lens in your eye focuses those rays to a point, which hits your retina. Your retina is in the back of your eye directly behind your eye's lens. At this point, the cells of the retina translate the light that is picked up to nerve impulses.

Your brain interprets those impulses, and sees a pinpoint of light in the sky that we know as a star. This assumes, of course, that you have good distance vision. If you don't, your retina will translate the image as a blur.

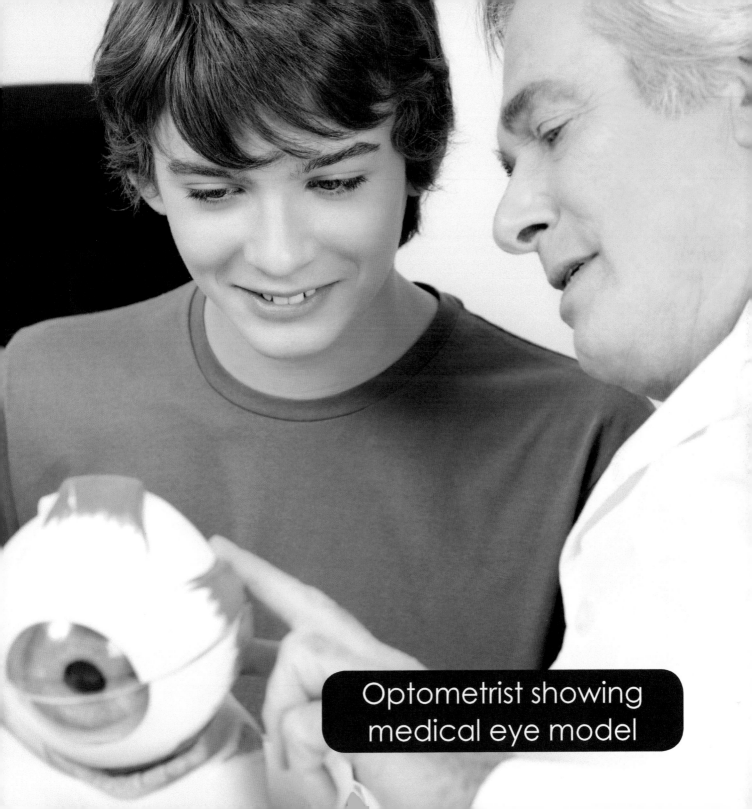

Optometrist showing
medical eye model

THE REFRACTING TELESCOPE

Suppose you're holding one of Galileo's refracting telescopes in your hands. The part that the light streams through, the aperture, is on the right. You'll eventually point that part toward a star or planet. The part on the left is the part you will look through to see the image. On the right, the light streams through the aperture to a convex primary lens.

For all practical purposes, you can assume that the individual light rays stream in parallel to each other. The primary or objective lens is curved just like the surface of your eye, so that it gathers light and brings it to a central point of focus. Now that the light is concentrated at a central point, it is much brighter than before.

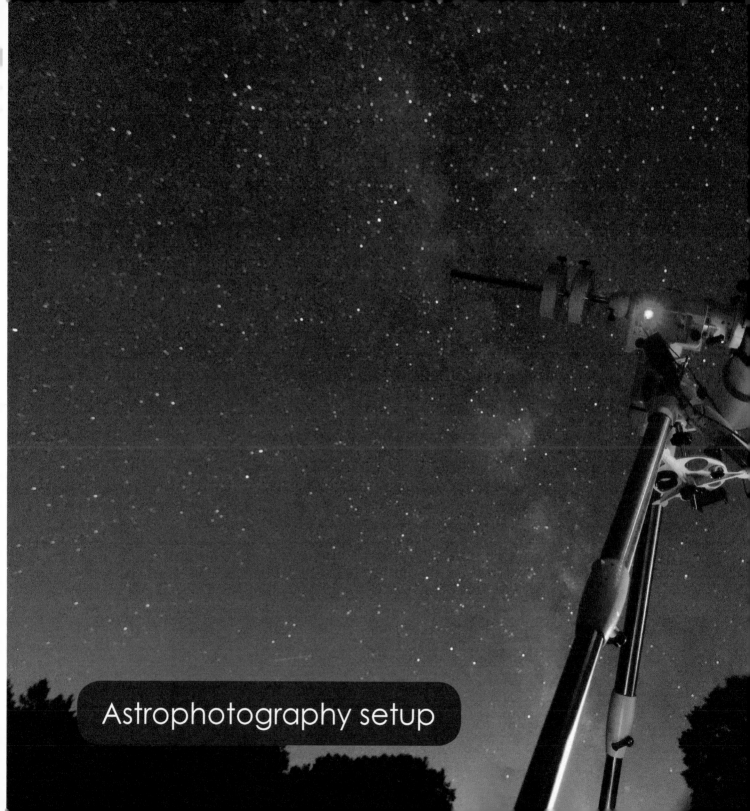

Astrophotography setup

This focal point is a real image that exists between the two lenses of the telescope, but now the telescope will convert it back to a virtual image that your eye can interpret. It hits a secondary eyepiece lens, which is a concave surface that spreads the light back to the size of your eye's pupil. This eyepiece acts as a magnifier. The light rays are parallel again now that they are coming back into your eye.

Now your eye goes about seeing the image the same way as it always does, except it will appear much larger than it appears if you try to look at it without the telescope. Using the telescope, you can see stars and planets that were very faint, because the telescope has concentrated the light. The larger that the primary lens is, the more light it will gather, and the more you'll be able to see.

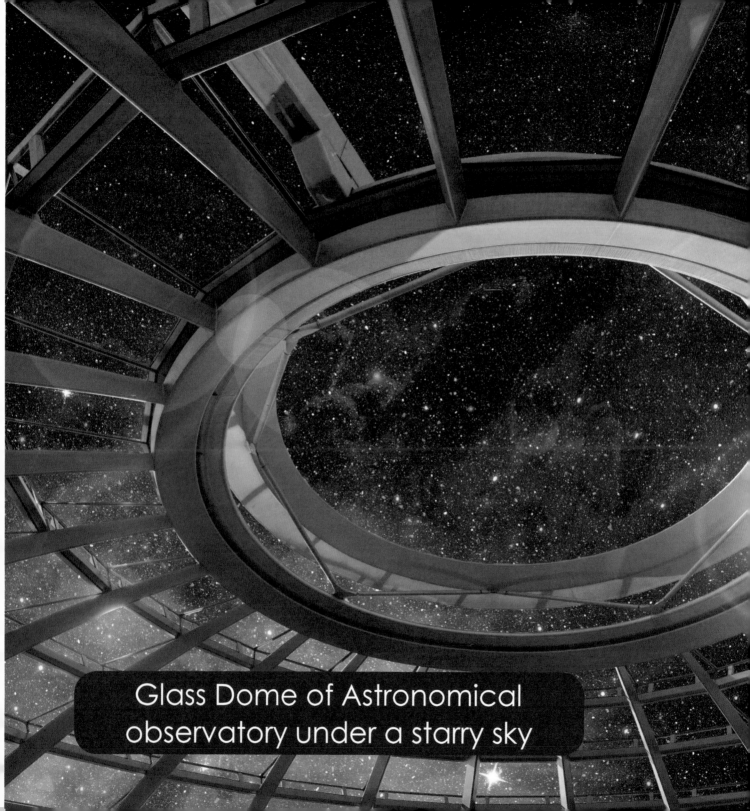

Glass Dome of Astronomical observatory under a starry sky

The focal length of the telescope and the magnification power of the eyepiece will determine how magnified the object you see will be. In most modern telescopes, the eyepieces can be changed out for different levels of magnification. In a way, the telescope is acting like a giant eye for you.

Man using the modern
Newtonian telescope

THE REFLECTING TELESCOPE

The reflecting telescope design that was created by Isaac Newton is still being used today. This type of telescope uses mirrors instead of lenses. A convex mirror gathers the light. Then it reflects that gathered light to a focal point. A second mirror is used to channel the light to a magnifying eyepiece.

WHAT CAN YOU SEE WITH A HOBBY TELESCOPE?

Depending on how much light there is in your area, you'll be able to see quite a bit with a hobby telescope. The darker it is out, and the cleaner your air is, the better you'll be able to see.

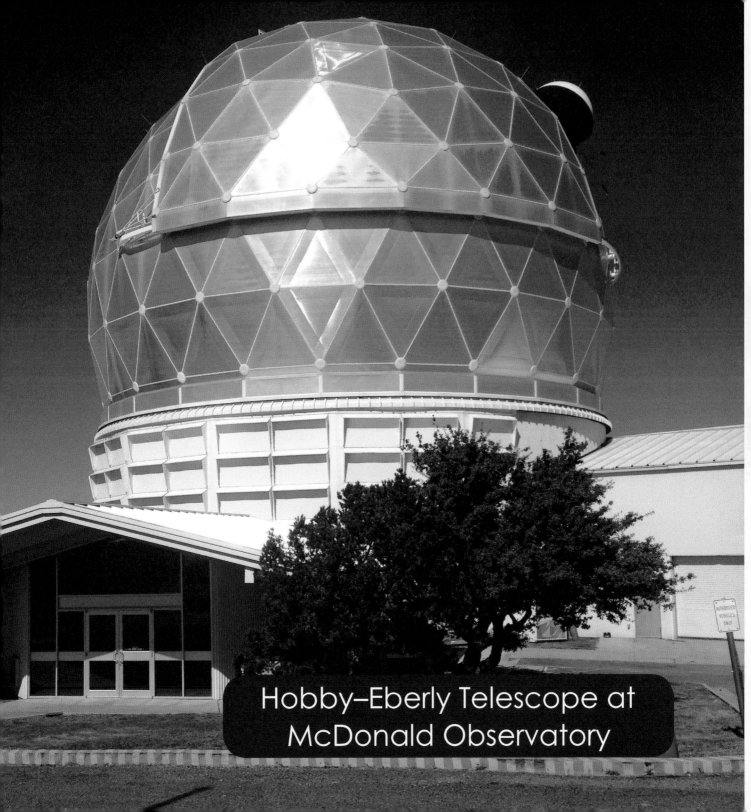

Hobby–Eberly Telescope at McDonald Observatory

The Planet Jupiter

Through a large, high-quality telescope at about 300X power magnification, you'll be able to see a lot of detail on the surface of the moon. You'll also be able to see Mars, Jupiter, and Saturn and some of their moons. You'll be able to see the phases of Venus and Mercury.

Neptune and Uranus are so far away that you'll only be able to see them as blue or green disks. On the other hand, you'll be able to see deep sky objects, such as the Swan Nebula, the Pinwheel Galaxy, or the Hercules Cluster, quite well if you live in an area that doesn't have too much pollution.

The Magellanic Cloud

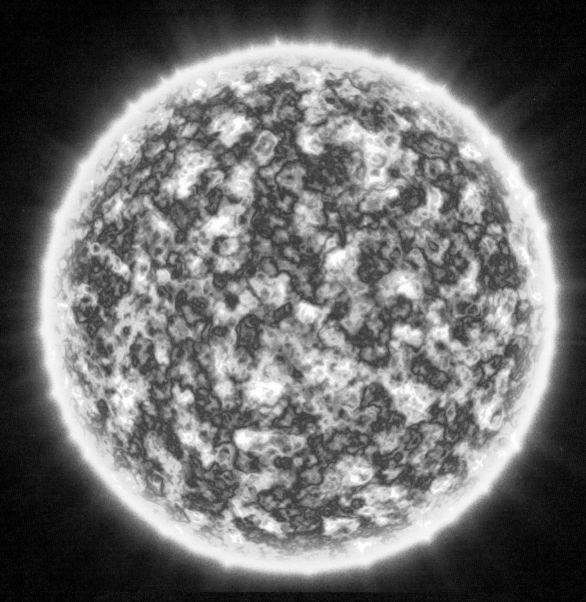

Close up view of the Sun

You can't observe the Sun directly unless you have a special type of filter. You can get solar filters or hydrogen alpha filters and these will allow you to view the Sun. Sunspots peak on a cycle that occurs every 11 years. If you buy an alpha filter, you'll be able to see prominences. These are large bright features that extend off the Sun's surface.

THE HUBBLE SPACE TELESCOPE

The famous Hubble Space Telescope is a reflecting telescope. It was launched into space by the Space Station. Shortly after it was launched and started sending information back to Earth, it was discovered that there was a problem.

Hubble Space Telescope

Space Satellite in Orbit

Its primary mirror was flawed. It had a flaw that made it off by 1/50 of the thickness of a sheet of paper. It had cost over 1.5 billion dollars to launch the Hubble so something had to be done, otherwise there would be no sharp pictures from space.

It took three years for NASA to determine how to correct the situation. With a series of small mirrors, they corrected the problem. It was almost as if they had put a contact lens on Hubble's eye!

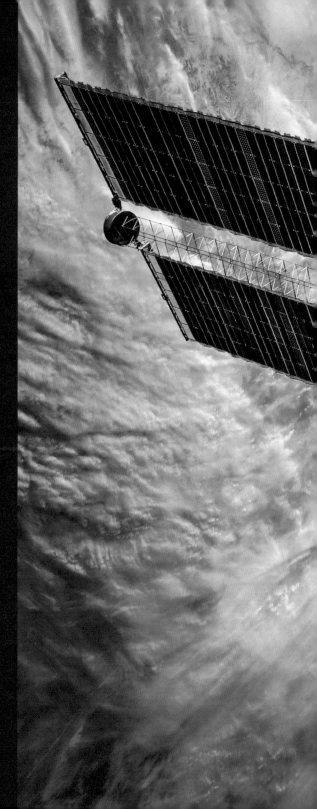

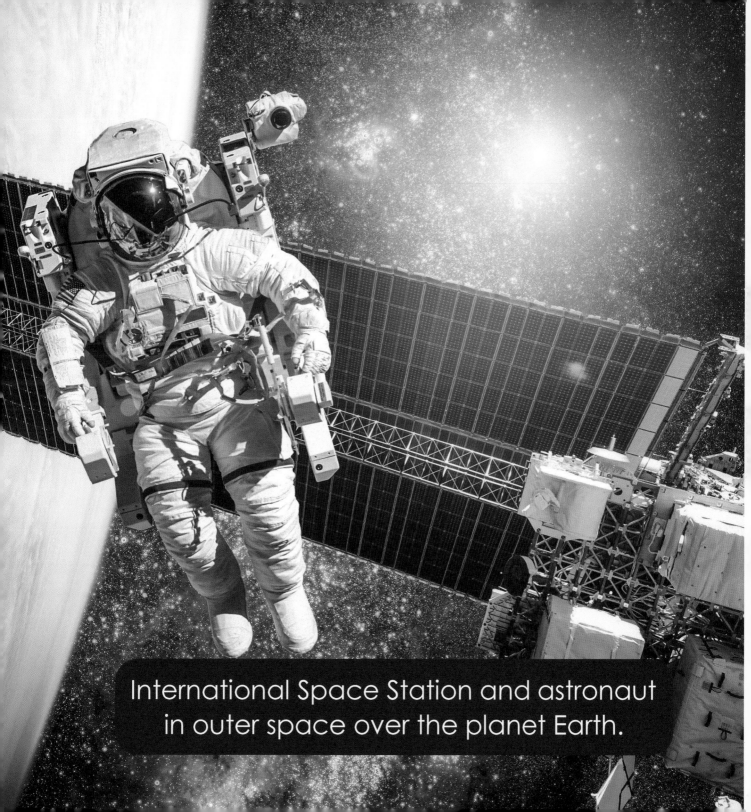

International Space Station and astronaut in outer space over the planet Earth.

Hubble takes a picture of Mars during a close approach

The new images that Hubble streamed back were spectacular. The magnification of the Hubble Telescope is 4700X and it can see much further into space than Earth-bound telescopes since it doesn't have to look through Earth's atmosphere.

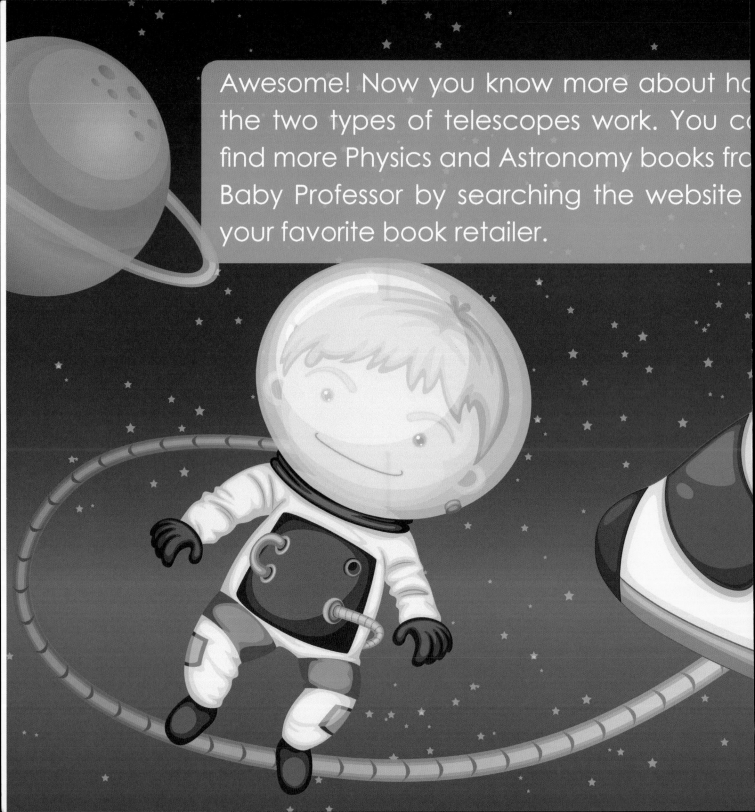

Awesome! Now you know more about how the two types of telescopes work. You can find more Physics and Astronomy books from Baby Professor by searching the website of your favorite book retailer.

Visit

BABY PROFESSOR
EDUCATION KIDS

www.BabyProfessorBooks.com

to download Free Baby Professor eBooks and view
our catalog of new and exciting Children's Books

Printed in Great
Britain
by Amazon